US Destroyers

in action

By Al Adcock

Color by Don Greer

Illustrated by David Gebhardt and Darren Glenn

Part 3

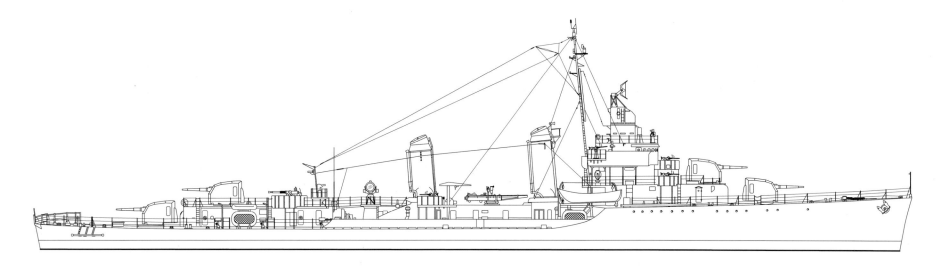

Warships Number 21

squadron/signal publications

USS THORN (DD-647) engages the Japanese destroyer ASAGUMO in the Surigao Strait, the Philippines early in the morning of 26 October 1944. The LIVERMORE Class destroyer torpedoed ASAGUMO, which was then sunk by the cruiser USS DENVER (CL-58). THORN was assigned to Destroyer Squadron Nineteen (DesRon 19) and was camouflaged in Measure 31/16D, the Dark Pattern System. She earned seven Battle Stars for her actions in the Pacific during World War Two.

Acknowledgements

All of the photos used in this publication are Official US Navy, declassified and provided by the following photo archivists and Veterans of the US Navy:

Real War Photos	Thomas C. Edrington III	USS THORN Association
Floating Drydock	Naval Historical Center	James Diamond
US Navy	National Archives	W.A. Wisnowski

Author's Note:

The Class layout in this publication is in accordance with James C. Fahey's "The Ships and Aircraft of the US Fleet," 1942 War Edition and 1945 Victory Edition. I owe a particular debt of gratitude to the late Mr. Fahey for his insight in publishing his 'little blue bibles.' The first book I ever purchased on my own was the 1945 Victory Edition that I paid one US dollar for in 1949.

FS numbers were developed <u>after</u> World War Two and their use here is solely an approximation.

Dedication:

In memory of George Chizmar, owner of Real War Photos. His wife Lolita will continue in his life's work of providing quality images from his collection of the many wars that have been photographed.

ISBN 0-89747-473-2

If you have any photographs of aircraft, armor, soldiers or ships of any nation, particularly wartime snapshots, why not share them with us and help make Squadron/Signal's books all the more interesting and complete in the future. Any photograph sent to us will be copied and the original returned. The donor will be fully credited for any photos used. Please send them to:

Squadron/Signal Publications, Inc.
1115 Crowley Drive
Carrollton, TX 75011-5010

Если у вас есть фотографии самолётов, вооружения, солдат или кораблей любой страны, особенно, снимки времён войны, поделитесь с нами и помогите сделать новые книги издательства Эскадрон/Сигнал ещё интереснее. Мы переснимем ваши фотографии и вернём оригиналы. Имена приславших снимки будут сопровождать все опубликованные фотографии. Пожалуйста, присылайте фотографии по адресу:

Squadron/Signal Publications, Inc.
1115 Crowley Drive
Carrollton, TX 75011-5010

軍用機、装甲車両、兵士、軍艦などの写真を所持しておられる方はいらっしゃいませんか？どの国のものでも結構です。作戦中に撮影されたものが特に良いのです。Squadron/Signal社の出版する刊行物において、このような写真は内容を一層充実し、興味深くすることができます。当方にお送り頂いた写真は、複写の後お返しいたします。出版物中に写真を使用した場合は、必ず提供者のお名前を明記させて頂きます。お写真は下記にご送付ください。

Squadron/Signal Publications, Inc.
1115 Crowley Drive
Carrollton, TX 75011-5010

USS CORRY (DD-463) was finished in a modified Measure 12 camouflage scheme in 1942. This scheme used Navy Blue (5-N), Ocean Gray (5-O), and Haze Gray (5-H) on the vertical surfaces. This LIVERMORE Class destroyer sank the German submarine U-801 on 16 March 1944. A German mine sank CORRY off Utah Beach at Normandy, France on D-Day – 6 June 1944. She earned four Battle Stars for her service in the Atlantic. (Floating Drydock)

Introduction

The destroyer has been identified for the last 100 years as the protector of the fleet, screening the battleships, cruisers, and aircraft carriers from harm. Their role was expanded in the Atlantic and Pacific during World War Two to include hunting submarines, radar picket duty, anti-aircraft protection and escorting convoys.

The London Naval Conference of 1930 specified tonnage and the number of warships that could be constructed per year. It limited destroyer forces to a total of 150,000 tons[1] in commission and limited new construction to 1500 tons (1524 MT), although 16 percent of the total could be 1850 tons (1880 MT). After this treaty was signed, the US Navy was obliged to scrap 93 of the earlier 1000 ton (1016 MT) 'flush deck, four pipe' destroyers.

The US had over 300 destroyers in commission following the First World War – the largest destroyer force of any navy. In fact, the US Navy had more destroyers than available personnel for these vessels. The flush deck destroyers were converted into Destroyer Minelayers (DM) and Destroyer Minesweepers (DMS) to take advantage of available hulls. Six of the flush deckers were converted to High Speed Transports (APD) between 1938 and 1940. This conversion total increased to 36 ships by 1943 and these served during the 'Island Hopping' campaign in the Pacific.

All of the between the wars new construction US destroyers were armed with the new dual-purpose 5-inch (127MM)/38 caliber Mk 12 naval gun. This new weapon – able to engage both surface and aerial targets – first appeared on the 1931-1932 FARRAGUT Class (DD-348). The 5-inch/38 Mk 12 fired a 55-pound (25 KG) projectile to a maximum range of 18,200 yards

[1]Ton in this book is the long ton of 2240 pounds (1016 KG).

(16,642 M) at a 45° elevation. In the anti-aircraft role, this gun's ceiling was 37,200 feet (11,339 M) at an 85° elevation.

The FARRAGUT Class were the first new construction of destroyers in the US since 1922, when the last of the flush deckers were commissioned. The US had constructed 36 of the 1500 tonners and eight of the 1850 tonners by 1937. The destroyers were also armed with 21-inch (533MM) Mk 15 torpedoes in three, four, or five tube mounts. The 24-foot (7.3 M) long Mk 15 weighed 3841 pounds (1742 KG), including an 825-pound (374 KG) Torpex warhead. This torpedo had a maximum speed of 45 knots (52 MPH/83 KMH) and a maximum range of 15,000 yards (13,716 M) at 26.5 knots (31 MPH/49 KMH).

Initially, the destroyers were armed with the 1.1-inch (28MM) Mk 1 quad mounted machine gun for anti-aircraft defense. Each gun fired a 0.9-pound (0.4 KG) projectile up to 7400 yards (6767 M) at a 40° elevation and up to 19,000 feet (5791 M) at a 90° elevation. Maximum rate of fire was 150 rounds per minute. Mechanical unreliability and early war experience necessitated the 1.1-inch guns' removal in favor of the 40MM Bofors Mk 1/2 cannon in single, twin, or quad mounts from mid-1942. The Mk 1 (left hand gun) and Mk 2 (right-hand gun) fired a 2-pound (0.9 KG) projectile out to 11,000 yards (10,058 M) at a 42° elevation or up to 22,800 feet (6949 M) at a 90° elevation. It had a maximum firing rate of 160 rounds per minute.

The water-cooled 0.50 caliber (12.7 MM) Browning M2 machine gun rounded out the anti-aircraft protection. This gun fired a 1.6-ounce (45.4 G) projectile out to 7400 yards (6767 M) and up to a ceiling of 15,000 feet (4572 M). The M2's rate of fire was 550 to 700 rounds per minute. The .50 caliber weapon was replaced by the 20MM Oerlikon cannon in single or twin mounts from late 1941. The Oerlikon weapon fired a 0.3 pound (0.1 KG) shell to a maximum range of 4800 yards (4389 M) and a ceiling of 10,000 feet (3048 M). Its firing rate was 450 rounds per minute.

USS TALBOT (TB-15) was a torpedo boat built in 1897. It was employed in the ocean escort role and served as a test boat for fuel oil trials in 1900. TALBOT was armed with a single 1-pounder gun aft and two centerline 18-inch (457MM) torpedo tubes: one forward and one aft. (National Archives)

USS BARRY (DD-2) was the second US destroyer. Launched in 1902, she spent the majority of her career stationed in the Philippines. BARRY had a raised forecastle deck and was armed with two 3-inch (76MM)/25 caliber guns, five 6-pounders, and a pair of 18-inch torpedo tubes. (National Archives)

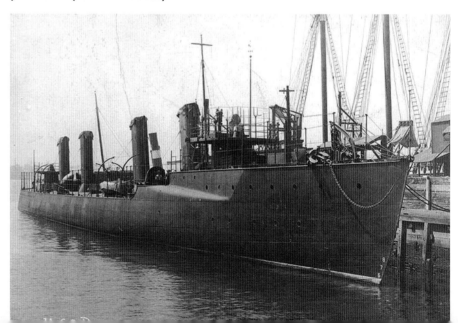

Two depth charge roller tracks were fitted to the fantail for Anti-Submarine Warfare (ASW). The 420-pound (191 KG) ashcan-shaped Mk 6 depth charge had a 300-pound (136 KG) charge and was effective at depths to 600 feet (183 M). The teardrop-shaped Mk 9 entered service in 1943. This had a 200-pound (91 KG) charge and was effective at depths down to 1000 feet (305 M). Either one or two four-tank smoke generators were fitted between or outside of the depth charge roller tracks. A destroyer generated smoke to screen their ship and others from enemy eyes.

US destroyers carried a variety of camouflage measures from their commissioning in the 1930s until the end of World War Two in August of 1945. Most vessels were painted in Measure 3, the Light Gray (5-L) System, when they were first commissioned. This was the standard measure for most US warships prior to World War Two. Various camouflage experiments in 1939 and 1940 introduced Measure 1, the Dark Gray System, and many 1850-ton SOMERS Class destroyers were painted in this scheme. Measure 1 used Dark Gray (5-D) on horizontal surfaces up to the exhaust stack top edge level and Light Gray above the exhausts. Other camouflage systems employed on US destroyers during the war included: Measure 21, the Navy Blue (5-N) System; Measure 22, the Graded System of Navy Blue on the lower hull and Haze Gray (5-H) on the upper hull and superstructure; and Measures 31 and 32 Pattern Systems.

During 1942, most US destroyers were camouflaged in either Measure 12, or Measure 12 (modified) – widely interpreted by shipyard painters with no two schemes being the same – or Measure 22. Measure 12 employed Ocean Gray (5-O), Haze Gray, and Navy Blue in a disruptive pattern. The Measure 16, Thayer Blue scheme adapted from the British 'Western Approaches' system was tried on a few SOMERS Class ships in the North Atlantic during 1943, with varying success. This scheme employed White (5-U) and Thayer Blue (5-B) in a disruptive pattern. It was common practice during 1944-45 to camouflage all of the destroyers in a division or squadron in all of the same camouflage measure. This made it difficult for enemy observers to determine the ships' names and movements.

The SC or SA air-search and SG surface radar sets were installed, as they became available to increase awareness of enemy threats in the air and on the surface. The SA radar was substituted when SC sets were unavailable. The SG set was also employed for navigation in inclement weather. Mk 51 optical and Mk 52 optical/radar controlled directors were fitted to control the 40MM mounts. The Mk 33 fire control system was employed on the SOMERS Class and the Mk 37 with radar control was fitted to the balance of the pre-war destroyers. DAVIS (DD-395) and JOUETT (DD-396) were also fitted with the Mk 37 fire control system when they were rebuilt in 1944.

The US Navy lost 24 of these between the wars destroyers during World War Two. These ships sunk included one in the SOMERS Class, two in the McCALL Class, five in the SIMS Class, three in the BENSON Class, and 13 in the LIVERMORE Class.

Twenty of the LIVERMORE Class were converted into High Speed Minesweepers (DMS) beginning in 1944. The conversion included removing the Number Four, 5-inch mount and all torpedo tubes. Sweep gear was added to the fantail in place of the 5-inch mount.

US Destroyers were named for US Navy heroes, people important to the development of US Naval forces, and for former destroyers so named.

USS FARQUHAR (DD-304) was a late CLEMSON Class 'flush-deck' destroyer that was commissioned following the First World War. She was armed with four 4-inch (102MM)/50 guns, one 3-inch/23 gun, and twelve 21-inch (533MM) torpedo tubes in four triple tube mounts. FARQUHAR was stricken in 1930 to comply with the London Naval Disarmament Treaty. (National Archives)

USS FARRAGUT (DD-348) represented a new class and design of US destroyers. They were armed with four of the new 5-inch (127MM)/38 caliber dual-purpose naval cannon and eight 21-inch torpedo tubes in four twin tube mounts. The eight FARRAGUT Class ships were constructed under the terms of the 1930 London Naval Treaty, which restricted displacement to 1500 tons. (National Archives)

Development

SOMERS Class

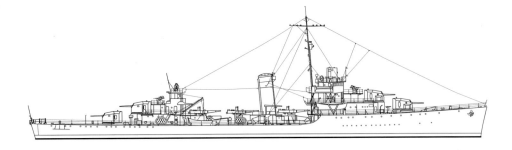

BENSON Class

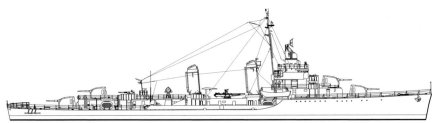

McCALL Class

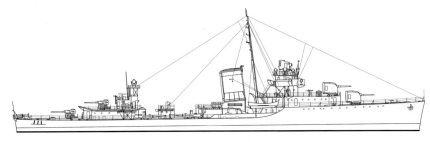

LIVERMORE Class

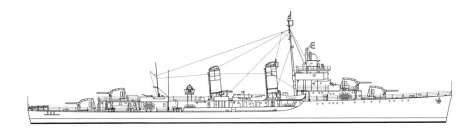

SIMS Class

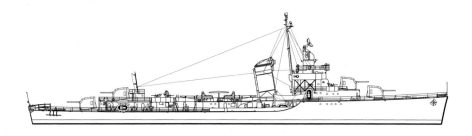

ELLYSON Class (DMS)

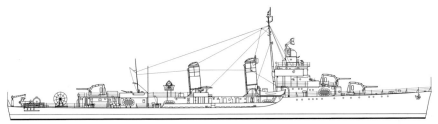

SOMERS Class of 1934-1935

The SOMERS Class consisted of five ships that were designed as Destroyer Leaders and designated as Heavy Destroyers. They were a development of the earlier PORTER Class of 1933, with a single funnel to make room for the extraordinary torpedo armament and quarters for Squadron Commanders and their staff. Their tonnage was determined by the 1930 London Naval Conference, as with all between the wars destroyers.

Each SOMERS Class ship was 381 feet 6 inches (116.3 M) in overall length and 372 feet (113.4 M) at the waterline. The beam was 36 feet 10.25 inches (11.2 M), while the standard draft was 11 feet 11 inches (3.6 M) and the full load draft was 13 feet 5.25 inches (4.1 M). Its standard displacement was rated at 1850 tons (1880 MT) and full war load displacement was 2767 tons (2811 MT). Four high-pressure Babcock & Wilcox boilers provided high temperature steam to the two General Electric geared turbines. Total available horsepower was rated at 52,000, which provided for a speed of 39 knots (45 MPH/72.3 KMH) at a displacement of 2140 tons (2174 MT). Range, with available onboard fuel of 627 tons (637 MT) was 7500 miles (12,070 KM) at 15 knots (17.3 MPH/27.8 KMH). The SOMERS Class had provisions for refueling at sea from an oiler or other ships so equipped to refuel while underway.

The SOMERS Class was originally armed with eight 5-inch (127MM)/38 caliber naval guns in four twin mounts: two forward and two aft. Initially, the 5-inch guns were directed by the optically sighted Mk 33 director. Radar was added by 1942 to increase accuracy during inclement weather or at night. War experience and inherent top-heavy conditions necessitated removing either the number two or three 5-inch mount and replacing it with a twin mount 40MM Bofors anti-aircraft cannon or a single mount 5-inch/38, depending on the ship. The pair of water-cooled 0.50 caliber (12.7 MM) machine guns and the two 1.1-inch (28MM) quad machine guns were soon replaced by the Oerlikon 20MM and Bofors 40MM cannons. Final war armament changes comprised either four or six 5-inch/38, a single mount 5-inch/38, fourteen 40MM in twin mounts and a pair of twin 20MM cannons. As constructed, the SOMERS Class was armed with twelve 21-inch (533MM) torpedo tubes in three quad mounts making them the most heavily armed destroyers in the world at the time. The torpedo armament was eventually reduced by removing and beaching the number two mount to add space for additional 40MM anti-aircraft armament in a continuing effort to decrease top weight. A pair of depth charge roller tracks fitted to the fantail completed the armament suite.

The SOMERS Class consisted of the Class leader SOMERS (DD-381), WARRINGTON (DD-383), SAMPSON (DD-394), DAVIS (DD-395), and JOUETT (DD-396). All were eventually assigned to Destroyers, Battle Force at San Diego, California by 1939. SOMERS served as Flagship of Destroyer Squadron Six (DesRon 6) and SAMPSON as Flagship of Destroyer Squadron Nine (DesRon 9). Upon completion of work up and training in 1938, WARRINGTON was assigned to Destroyer Squadron Ten (DesRon 10) in the Atlantic, but was later transferred to DesRon 6 in the Pacific.

DAVIS and JOUETT were rebuilt in 1944 and following reconstruction closely resembled the RUDDEROW Class of Destroyer Escorts. The conversions consisted of landing the number two and three twin 5-inch mounts and replacing them with twin 40MM mounts. Four additional twin 40MM mounts were also installed and the 20MM armament was increased to seven weapons. A Mk 37, Mod 17 gun director with Mk 12 and Mk 22 radar replaced the Mk 33 director. A High Frequency/Direction Finding (HF/DF) 'Huff/Duff' submarine hunting antenna replaced the main mast and a Direction Finding navigation antenna was placed on the stack.

USS SOMERS (DD-381) was the lead ship in 1934-1935 Class of 'heavy destroyers' or Destroyer Leaders. These ships were designed for use by Squadron Commanders and their staffs. The SOMERS Class ships were armed with eight 5-inch/38 guns in four twin mounts and three four-tube torpedo tube mounts. SOMERS is painted in Measure 3, the Light Gray System. (Real War Photos)

In 1944, SOMERS was camouflaged in Measure 32/3D, the Medium Pattern System designed for many destroyers built prior to the war. She earned two Battle Stars for her actions in the Atlantic escorting convoys and hunting German blockade-runners. SOMERS' main armament was reduced to six 5-inch guns and two torpedo tube mounts. (National Archives)

USS WARRINGTON (DD-383) was assigned to the Atlantic Fleet after her commissioning in 1938. In 1939, she was posted as the Flagship of Destroyer Squadron 6, Battle Force, Destroyers at San Diego, California. Damage from a hurricane resulted in WARRINGTON's loss off the Bahama Islands on 13 September 1944. She earned two Battle Stars for her wartime service. (Floating Drydock)

They finished out the war camouflaged in Measure 32/3D, the Medium Pattern System.

There was one loss for the class. WARRINGTON again assigned to the Atlantic fleet foundered and sank during a hurricane off the Bahama Islands on 13 September 1944. She had earned two Battle Stars for her service.

(Below) USS SAMPSON (DD-394) was camouflaged in the Thayer Blue Measure 16 blue and white scheme designed for the North Atlantic Western Approaches in 1943. SA air-search and SG surface search radar antennas are mounted on her foremast. Anti-aircraft armament was increased with the addition of 20MM and 40MM cannon, while the main armament was reduced to six 5-inch guns. (Real War Photos)

5-inch (127MM)/38 Caliber Twin Mount

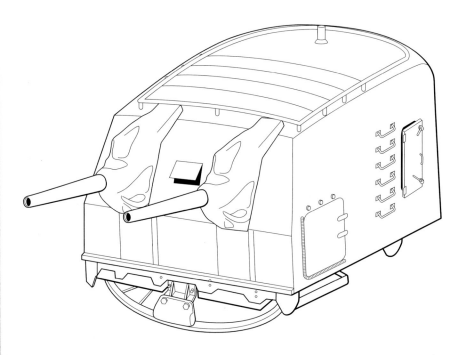

USS DAVIS (DD-395) was constructed by Bath Iron Works in Maine and commissioned in 1938. The Number Two twin 5-inch mount is trained to starboard following direction from the optical sighted Mk 33 gun director. A crow's nest lookout is fitted halfway up the foremast. DAVIS is painted in Measure 3, the Light Gray System that was standard for the US fleet in the late 1930s.

In 1944, DAVIS was rebuilt by reducing the size of the bridge and adding a Mk 37 Mod 17 radar controlled director to its roof. The main armament was a pair of twin 5-inch/38 twin mounts and a 5-inch/38 single mount replacing the Number Three twin mount. An FM whip antenna and a Direction Finding (DF) antenna were fitted to the stack and a High Frequency/Direction Finding (HF/DF, or 'huff/duff') antenna was placed atop the pole mainmast. When the conversion was completed, DAVIS resembled the RUDDEROW Class of destroyer escorts. (Floating Drydock)

USS JOUETT (DD-396) is in the process of dropping the starboard side anchor in 1938. The 'black ball' flying from the foremast indicates a ship at anchor and for ships approaching to lie to (not approach). JOUETT served in the Atlantic during the Second World War escorting convoys, participating in the Normandy Invasion, and performing anti-submarine duties. She earned three Battle Stars for her flag. (Floating Drydock)

USS BENHAM (DD-397) lies at anchor off New York City in 1939. She is painted in camouflage Measure 3, the Light Gray System. The middle half of the foremast is painted black to hide stack gas stains. Japanese destroyer torpedoes sank BENHAM during the Second Battle of Guadalcanal on 15 November 1942. (National Archives)

BENHAM rescues survivors of the mortally wounded aircraft carrier USS YORKTOWN (CV-5) during the Battle of Midway on 7 June 1942. YORKTOWN lists to port and soon sank from the effects of Japanese submarine torpedo hits. BENHAM is camouflaged in Measure 21, the Navy Blue System. (National Archives)

McCALL Class of 1935

The McCALL Class, like the SOMERS Class, was constructed under the terms of the 1930s London Naval Conference that limited the per year tonnage on destroyers. The treaty also applied to all other warships. The terms also specified the armament on destroyers not to exceed a bore diameter of 5-inches (127MM). Twelve McCALL Class destroyers were built and commissioned by 1939.

The McCALL Class was designed by two different naval architects, with Bethlehem, San Francisco designing the class leader McCALL (DD-400) and MAURY (DD-401) and Gibbs & Cox the ten remaining ships. The Bethlehem designed destroyers were unique in having flat-sided stacks, while the others featured rounded stacks. All were designed with a standard displacement of 1500 tons (1524 MT), a main armament of 5-inch guns, and 12 torpedo tubes.

The McCALL Class was 341 feet 4.25 inches (104 M) in overall length and 334 feet (101.8 M) at the waterline. Beam was 35 feet 6.5 inches (10.8 M) and standard draft of 11 feet 1.5 inches (3.4 M) and full wartime draft of 12 feet 8.5 inches (3.9 M). Power was produced by three super-heated, high-pressure (650-pound/295 KG) Babcock & Wilcox boilers that provided steam to the two Westinghouse geared turbines. A total of 50,000 shaft horsepower available to the twin screws enabled the class to achieve over 40 knots (46 MPH/74 KMH) on trials. Range with onboard fuel of 484 tons (492 MT) was 8000 miles (12,874 KM) at 12 knots (13.8 MPH/22.2 KMH). The McCALL Class, like all other US destroyers were capable of underway refueling to extend their range. Standard displacement was rated at 1500 tons (1524 MT) and maximum full war load rating was 2219 tons (2255 MT).

Armament on the McCALL class consisted of four 5-inch (127MM)/38 single mount dual-purpose naval guns, with the two forward mounts (number 1 and 2) enclosed and the two aft mounts (Numbers 3 and 4) open. LANG (DD-399) was fitted with the two aft mounts enclosed in 1942, but reverted back to open mounts the next year. The original secondary anti-aircraft armament was the 1.1-inch (28MM) machine gun in a quad mount. This gun was found to be inadequate in service and was soon replaced by the 40MM Bofors cannon in twin mounts. A pair of water-cooled 0.50 caliber (12.7MM) Browning machine guns rounded out the defensive armament. The 0.50 caliber was soon replaced by the 20MM Oerlikon cannon, first in a single mount and by 1945, twin mounts. Torpedo armament consisted of twelve 21-inch torpedo tubes in four mounts, two per side. By 1942, the two aft sets of tubes (Numbers 3 and 4) were beached in favor of a pair of 40MM cannon. The beached tubes soon found their way onto Destroyer Escorts (DEs). Two depth charge roller tracks were fitted to the fantail for Anti-Submarine Warfare (ASW).

There were two losses in the class, with the first occurring during the night of 15 November 1942 off of Guadalcanal when BENHAM (DD-397) was torpedoed while in support of Task Force 64. Not a single crewman was lost on the BENHAM during this action in the Pacific. BENHAM had earned five Battle Stars for her service. The second loss occurred on 11 September 1943 in the Mediterranean off of Salerno, Italy when ROWAN (DD-405) was attacked by German *schnellboote* ('E-Boats'[1]) that put a torpedo into her port quarter causing irreparable damage, and the loss of 202 officers and men. ROWAN earned five Battle Stars for her flag for her service in the Atlantic.

---

[1] A *schnellboot* (fast boat) was a German motor torpedo vessel, equivalent to an American PT boat or British MTB. The Allies referred to *schnellboote* as 'E-Boats' (for Enemy Boats).

USS ELLET (DD-398) pulls up alongside of the Amphibious Force Flagship USS APPALACHIAN (AGC-1) to deliver classified guard mail (secure written communications) on 7 January 1944. ELLET is camouflaged in Measure 21. The mainmast is fitted with SA air-search and SG sea search radar. The Mk 12 radar antenna mounted to the front of the Mk 37 gun director helped reduce top weight. (Real War Photos)

USS LANG (DD-399) is underway in the Atlantic camouflaged in a modified Measure 12 on 26 May 1942, shortly before her transfer to the Pacific. She earned 11 Battle Stars for her service in the Pacific. LANG was one of a few McCALL Class destroyers to have four enclosed 5-inch mounts. (National Archives)

The class leader USS McCALL (DD-400) pulls up along the starboard side of the carrier ENTERPRISE (CV-6) to refuel in a rough sea on 18 November 1941. This was a few days before the Japanese attack on Pearl Harbor. McCALL is still fitted with the large search-light platform on the mid deck. She earned nine Battle Stars for her Pacific service. (Real War Photos)

5-Inch (127mm)/38 Caliber Single Enclosed Mount

5-Inch/38 Caliber Single Open Mount

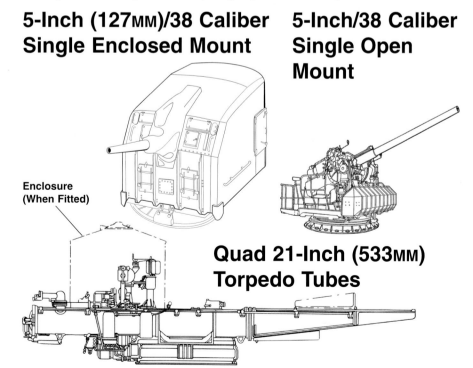

Enclosure
(When Fitted)

Quad 21-Inch (533mm) Torpedo Tubes

USS MAURY (DD-401) flies the Bethlehem house flag atop the foremast during trials in 1938, before her commissioning ceremonies. She is camouflaged in Measure 3, the US Navy's standard scheme before 1940. MAURY earned the Presidential Unit Citation and 16 Battle Stars for her flag for service in the Pacific. (National Archives)

USS STACK (DD-406) is painted in her pre-war Light Gray scheme in 1940. Like her sisters, STACK's two forward 5-inch guns are enclosed, while her aft two weapons are open. A Mk 33 director for these guns is located atop the bridge. Both the boot topping just above the waterline and the funnel top were painted Black. (US Navy)

USS RHIND (DD-404) steams in the Pacific in 1945. She is believed to be camouflaged in the Graded System, Measure 22. A Mk 28 radar antenna is fitted to the face of the Mk 33 gun director and an SG surface search antenna is atop the foremast. RHIND earned four Battle Stars for her Atlantic and Pacific service. (Floating Drydock)

US Navy Destroyer Colors of World War Two

(FS numbers were developed <u>after</u> World War Two and their use here is solely an approximation.)

Color Name	Approx. FS No.	Measures Used
Thayer Blue (5-B)	35450	16
Dark Gray (5-D)	36163	1
Haze Gray (5-H)	35237	12, 22, 31
Light Gray (5-L)	36320	1, 3, 32
Navy Blue (5-N)	35044	21, 22, 15
Navy Green (5-NG)	34128	31
Ocean Gray (5-O)	35164	12, 31, 32, 15
Ocean Green (5-OG)	34227	31
Sea Blue (5-S)	35045	11, 12
White (5-U)	37855	5, 16, 22, 15
Deck Blue (20-B)	35042	Most; For Decks & Other Horizontal Surfaces
Dull Black (#82, later BK)	37040	31, 32

USS ROWAN (DD-405), painted in the pre-war Measure 3 scheme, moves in a rolling sea in the late 1930s. German *schnellboote* ('E-Boats'; motor torpedo boats) sank her off Salerno, Italy on 11 September 1943. ROWAN earned five Battle Stars for her service in the Atlantic and Mediterranean Theaters. (Real War Photos)

USS TRIPPE (DD-403) moves at speed in the Atlantic on 9 July 1944. She is believed to be camouflaged in Measure 22. Mk 4 radar is fitted to the face of the Mk 33 director in an effort to save top weight. TRIPPE earned six Battle Stars for her Atlantic service and a brief time in the Pacific. (Real War Photos)

USS STERETT (DD-407) cruises alongside the escort carrier USS MARCUS ISLAND (CVE-77) in the South China Sea. The destroyer's camouflage is believed to be Measure 31/11D, the Dark Pattern System. The foremast contains SA-2 air-search and SG surface search antennas. The Number One and Two 5-inch mounts are fully enclosed while the Number Three and Four mounts are the open type. (National Archives)

13

1.1-Inch (28mm) Quad Mount

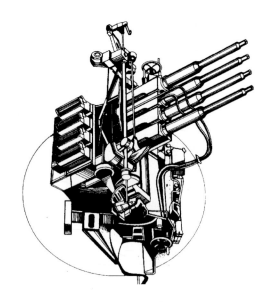

STACK moves slowly off Mare Island Navy Yard near San Francisco, California on 27 May 1944. She has just been refitted and is camouflaged in Measure 32/11D. A Mk 37 gun director with Mk 4 radar is mounted atop the bridge area. STACK earned 12 Battle Stars for her wartime service in the Pacific. (National Archives)

USS WILSON (DD-408) is camouflaged in Measure 21, the Navy Blue System, while steaming off the Mare Island Navy Yard on 2 December 1942. She is equipped with the Mk 37 gun director atop the bridge, and SA and SG radar antennas on the foremast. WILSON earned 11 Battle Stars for her service in the Pacific during World War Two. (National Archives)

20mm Single Mount Cannon

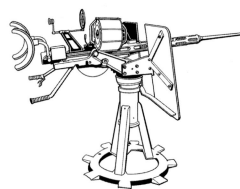

20mm Twin Mount Cannon

SIMS Class of 1936

The SIMS Class represented a new style of destroyer design with a rounded bridge super-structure and a rounded sheer line on the forecastle and the number two gun deck. This 'streamlining' was probably due to the wave of airplane and automobile styling in the 1930s that employed aerodynamics in their design. The naval architects were attempting to take advantage of reduced drag and thus higher speed from reduced friction in the ships.

The SIMS Class was 341 feet 4.25 inches (104 M) in length at the waterline and 348 feet 3.13 inches (106.1 M) in overall length. Beam was 36 feet 1.13 inches (11 M) and draft was rated at 12 feet 0.25 inch (3.7 M) standard and 12 feet 8.31 inches (3.9 M) maximum full war load. Power for the SIMS Class came from three Babcock & Wilcox boilers that provided high-pressure (800 PSI), high temperature (650°) steam to the pair of Westinghouse geared turbines. A total of 50,000 shaft horsepower (SHP) enabled the SIMS Class to achieve 38.5 knots (44.3 MPH/71.3 KMH) with light displacement; however, 35 knots (40.3 MPH/65 KMH) was the standard maximum speed. Displacement was 120 tons (121.9 MT) over the 1500 ton (1524 MT) treaty weight limit, which was due mainly to the additional 5-inch gun, torpedo tube, and the machinery plant. The SIMS displaced 1620 tons (1646 MT) standard and 2293 tons (2330 MT) at full war load. Range was 6500 nautical miles (7485 miles/12,045 KM) at 12 knots (13.8 MPH/22.2 KMH) with available onboard fuel of 460 tons (467 MT). This SIMS Class and other US destroyers could be refueled at sea by a tanker (AO) or any other ship equipped to dispense fuel while underway.

Armament on the SIMS was initially five of the dual-purpose 5-inch/38 naval guns, with the Numbers 1 ,2, and 5 mounts fully enclosed and the Numbers 3 and 4 open, mainly to save top weight. The new Mk 37 Gun Fire Control Director was fitted atop the bridge area to control the 5-inch (127MM) guns. Four of the water-cooled 0.50 caliber (12.7MM) machine guns were also fitted to provide anti-aircraft protection. Three four tube 21-inch (533MM) torpedo tubes were placed two on the main deck edge waist position and one abaft the stack on the center-line. In 1940 the torpedo tubes were arranged with the waist positions being eliminated and one of the tubes being placed on a new superstructure mounted on the centerline. This new arrangement retained the eight-tube broadside that twelve tube mounts offered. The beached tubes eventually were placed on the ATLANTA (CL-51) Class of light cruisers. War emergency anti-aircraft measures removed the Number Three 5-inch mount replacing it with a pair of 40MM mounts on a raised bandstand. A pair of depth charge roller tracks were fitted to the fan-tail for Anti-Submarine Warfare (ASW).

Six yards on the US East Coast built the 12 SIMS Class destroyers, which were all assigned to the Atlantic Fleet after they were commissioned. There were five losses in the SIMS Class including the class leader SIMS (DD-409). Japanese bombs sank SIMS during the Battle of the Coral Sea on 7 May 1942, but not before she downed five of the attacking aircraft. SIMS earned two Battle Stars for her service in the Pacific. The second loss occurred during the Battle of Midway, one month later, on 6 June 1942. HAMMANN (DD-412) became one of the two US ship losses suffered during that momentous battle, when she was struck by a Japanese torpedo launched by the I-168. The I-168 was also responsible for sinking the US carrier YORKTOWN (CV-5) during the battle. The third loss occurred south of the Solomon Islands, when the Japanese submarines I-15 and I-19 launched 61 CM (24 inch) Type 93 'long lance' torpedoes at O'BRIEN (DD-415) on 15 September 1942. One torpedo found its mark and blew off the bow. The damage was serious and she sailed toward Espiritu Santo for temporary

USS SIMS (DD-409) slowly moves during builder's trials out of Bath Iron Works in July of 1939. The new 'streamlined' look was added to her forecastle, Number Two gun deck, and bridge area. The Mk 37 fire control director has yet to be fitted atop the bridge. The class leader SIMS was painted in Measure 3, the Light Gray System. (National Archives)

Sailing off Mare Island Navy Yard on 1 August 1942, USS HUGHES (DD-410) is camou-flaged in a modified Measure 12 System. This scheme varied from ship-to-ship, with no two schemes being the same. HUGHES carries an SA air-search antenna atop her fore-mast and a Mk 37 fire control director atop her bridge area. (National Archives)

repairs. While sailing to Pearl Harbor on 19 October 1942, she broke up and sank off of the Samoan Islands, with no loss of any crewmen.

The fourth loss occurred off of Savo Island on 14 November 1942, when WALKE (DD-416) – serving with Task Force 64 – engaged the Japanese cruiser NAGARA. The destroyer scored several hits with her 5-inch guns before a torpedo and numerous 203mm (8-inch) rounds from NAGARA hit WALKE. She quickly sank into 'Ironbottom Sound,' so named for the many Allied and Japanese ships sunk in these waters. The final, and fifth, loss occurred in the Mediterranean, when two torpedoes launched by the German submarine U-616 hit BUCK (DD-420) patrolling off the mouth of the Gulf of Salerno on 9 October 1943. The torpedoes blew off her bow and caused the forward 5-inch magazine to explode. BUCK quickly sank with the loss of 150 of her crew. She had earned three Battle Stars for her service in both the Atlantic and Mediterranean. Following the Second World War, all of the remaining SIMS Class were stricken and scrapped.

USS ANDERSON (DD-411) moves alongside the carrier USS WASP (CV-7) during a Neutrality Patrol in the Atlantic. The hull numbers and ship's name on the fantail were painted out as a security precaution for her transiting the Panama Canal in 1941. ANDERSON is camouflaged in Measure 3, the Light Gray System. (National Archives)

ANDERSON shows off her sleek, aerodynamic lines while running builder's trials in 1939. She carries her full torpedo armament of 12 tubes in three quad mounts, but is not yet equipped with a Mk 37 fire control director on the bridge roof. The SIMS Class was capable of 38.5 knots (41.3 mph/71.3 kmh) in light displacement condition. (National Archives)

McCALL Class

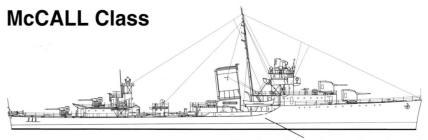

Flat sheer line on forecastle and gun deck

SIMS Class

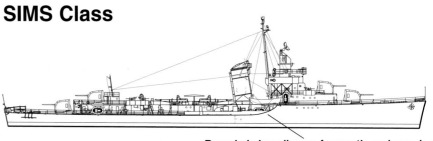

Rounded sheer line on forecastle and gun deck

USS HAMMANN (DD-412) shows off her pair of depth charge roller tracks and smoke generating equipment on the fantail. The aft superstructure contains the searchlight platform, a pair of boat handling cranes, and two open mount 5-inch/38 guns. The Japanese submarine I-168 sank HAMMANN during the Battle of Midway on 6 June 1942. She earned two Battle Stars for her actions during that battle and the earlier Battle of the Coral Sea. (National Archives)

A Curtiss SBC-3 Helldiver scout-bomber (6-S-5) flies past USS MUSTIN (DD-413) during exercises on 26 May 1940. The Helldiver was assigned to Scouting Squadron Six (VS-6) from the carrier USS ENTERPRISE (CV-6). She is painted in the Light Gray System of Measure 3, while the hull numbers were White with Black shadows. MUSTIN earned 13 Battle Stars for her extensive activities in the Pacific. (National Archives)

Mk 6 Depth Charge

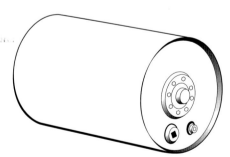

Mk 9 Depth Charge

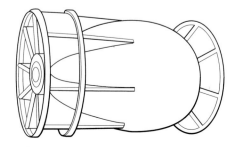

Roller Track

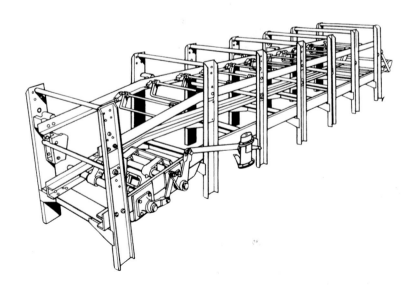

Smoke Generators

(Above) USS RUSSELL (DD-414) sails out of Newport News, Virginia following her commissioning ceremonies on 3 November 1939. RUSSELL was a veteran of the Battles of Coral Sea and Midway and earned 16 Battle Stars for her flag by war's end. She is painted in camouflage Measure 3. (Real War Photos)

(Left) MUSTIN stands out of Pearl Harbor, Hawaii on 14 June 1942. She is camouflaged in the modified Measure 12, a scheme that was different on every ship so painted. She missed the great Battle of Midway, as she was returning from convoy duty. MUSTIN has been refitted with four enclosed 5-inch/38 mounts. (National Archives)

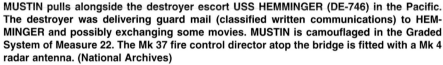

MUSTIN pulls alongside the destroyer escort USS HEMMINGER (DE-746) in the Pacific. The destroyer was delivering guard mail (classified written communications) to HEMMINGER and possibly exchanging some movies. MUSTIN is camouflaged in the Graded System of Measure 22. The Mk 37 fire control director atop the bridge is fitted with a Mk 4 radar antenna. (National Archives)

USS WALKE (DD-416) is painted in camouflage Measure 3, the Light Gray System in 1940. She participated in the Neutrality Patrols in the Atlantic in this scheme until transferring to the Pacific in late December of 1941. Staging boards over the hull side indicate the ship's 'rust gang' (corrosion-fighting crew) is paying attention to her paint finish. (National Archives)

USS O'BRIEN (DD-415), like her sisters, was armed with five 5-inch/38 guns. The Number One, Two, and Five mounts were enclosed, while the Number Three and Four mounts were open. Torpedoes fired from the Japanese submarines I-15 and I-19 severely damaged O'BRIEN on 15 September 1942. Damage from the attack caused her to split open and sink while returning to Pearl Harbor on 19 October 1942. (National Archives)

WALKE (DD-416) stands off the Mare Island Navy Yard on 24 August 1942, following a period in the yard. She is painted in modified camouflage Measure 12. Japanese torpedoes and gunfire sank WALKE during the Second Battle of Guadalcanal on 14 November 1942. She earned three Battle Stars for her Pacific service. (National Archives)

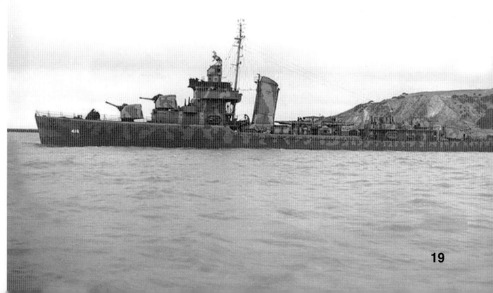

USS MORRIS (DD-417) is underway in the Pacific on 6 December 1943. She is camou-flaged in Measure 21, the Navy Blue System. MORRIS was the first US destroyer equipped with fire control radar on her Mk 37 director. She was a veteran of the Battles of the Coral Sea and Midway and earned 15 Battle Stars for her Pacific service. (Real War Photos)

The Charleston Navy Yard, South Carolina built USS ROE (DD-418) at a cost of over $4.25 million, less the cost of armament and other 'government furnished equipment.' She was camouflaged in a modified Measure 12 scheme in 1942. ROE earned six Battle Stars for her service in the Atlantic and Pacific during World War Two. (Real War Photos)

USS WAINWRIGHT (DD-419) shows off her new cam-ouflage, a modified Measure 12, while off the Norfolk Navy Yard, Virginia on 22 March 1942. She lacks her SA air-search and SG surface search radar antennas on her foremast. The Mk 4 radar for her Mk 37 fire control director atop the bridge has not been installed. WAINWRIGHT's main armament was reduced from five to four 5-inch/38 dual-purpose guns. Two 40MM Bofors cannon replaced her Number Three gun for improved anti-aircraft protection. WAINWRIGHT earned seven Battle Stars for her ser-vice in the Atlantic, Mediterranean, and Pacific. (Floating Drydock)

USS BUCK (DD-420) was constructed at the Philadelphia Navy Yard, Pennsylvania and commissioned on 15 May 1940. Her original armament consisted of five 5-inch/38 guns and eight 21-inch (533MM) torpedo tubes in two mounts of four tubes per mount. BUCK is painted in the Light Gray Measure 3 scheme. Hull numbers were white with black shadows. The portholes along her hull were plated over after the US entered World War Two in December of 1941. (Floating Drydock)

BUCK (DD-420) is camouflaged in a modified Measure 22 in the fall of 1943. This pattern differs from the one used on her sister ship ROE (DD-418). The German submarine U-616 sank BUCK in the Mediterranean off Salerno, Italy on 9 October 1943. She earned three Battle Stars for her service in the Atlantic and Mediterranean. (Real War Photos)

40MM Bofors Cannon

Single Mount

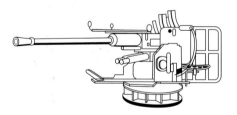

Twin Mount

Quad Mount

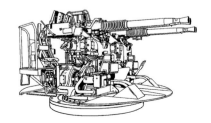

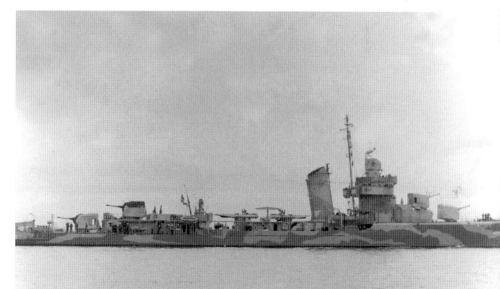

BENSON Class of 1937-1940

The 32 BENSON Class ships represented the last class of the pre-war destroyers. All these ships were constructed and commissioned by 1943, just in time to provide fleet security. They were constructed from plans drawn by Bethlehem with the exception of GLEAVES (DD-423) and NIBLACK (DD-424), which were constructed from plans prepared by Gibbs & Cox. The Bethlehem designed vessels had flat-sided funnels while the two 'odd' sisters were fitted with round stacks. The class layout was altered following World War Two by combining the newly established GLEAVES Class and LIVERMORE (DD-429) Class into one. Gibbs & Cox designed both the LIVERMORE and GLEAVES Classes.

The BENSON Class was 348 feet 1.81 inches (106.1 M) in length overall and 341 feet 3.38 inches (104 M) at the waterline. Beam was 36 feet 2.13 inches (11 M) and draft was rated at 12 feet 7.75 inches (3.9 M) standard and 13 feet 4.5 inches (4.1 M) at full war load. Standard displacement was 1840 tons (1870 MT) and full war load was 2474 tons (2514 MT). Maximum rated speed was 38 knots (43.8 MPH/70.4 KMH) made possible by the four Babcock & Wilcox boilers that provided high pressure, high temperature steam to the pair of Westinghouse geared turbines that drove the twin screws with a total of 50,000 SHP available. Her range was 5580 nautical miles (6425 miles/10,340 KM) at 12 knots (13.8 MPH/22.2 KMH).

Armament on the BENSON Class originally consisted of five 5-inch (127MM)/38 dual-purpose naval guns and four water-cooled 0.50 caliber (12.7MM) machine guns. The war in the Atlantic and British influence dictated that the number three 5-inch gun be landed and replaced by 40MM Bofors anti-aircraft cannon in a twin mount. As they became available, the Oerlikon 20MM cannon in single and eventually twin mounts replaced the 0.50 machine guns. The 5-inch guns were directed by the Mk 37 radar controlled fire director and the 40MM guns by either the Mk 51 or the radar enhanced Mk 52 director.

A single 21-inch (533MM) five-tube (quint) torpedo launcher was fitted between the twin stacks and one abaft the number two stack. The number two tubes were eventually beached in favor of increased 20MM and 40MM mounts. For anti-submarine duty, a pair of depth charge roller tracks were fitted at the fantail and four roller racks or 'k' gun depth charge throwers – two on each deck edge – rounded out the offensive and defensive armament.

There were three losses of the BENSON Class during World War Two with two of them occurring on the same night during the Battle of Savo Island on Friday, 13 November 1942. This day became known as 'Black Friday' for all the losses incurred by American naval forces. LAFFEY (DD-459) and BARTON (DD-599), along with the light cruisers ATLANTA (CL-51) and JUNEAU (CL-52) and destroyers CUSHING (DD-376) and MONSSEN (DD-436) were sunk during that fateful battle north of Guadalcanal. The Japanese were determined to destroy Henderson Field and retake the island and thus launched a naval attack with two battleships, a light cruiser, and 14 destroyers. The American forces were badly outnumbered and out-gunned during the night engagement that saw LAFFEY sunk by numerous 356MM (14-inch) rounds from the Japanese battleship HIEI and BARTON being hit by two torpedoes fired from a Japanese destroyer. When the battle was over and the score tallied the Japanese had lost the battleship HIEI and the destroyers AKATSUKI and YUDACHI, with the battleship KIRISHIMA severely damaged. (KIRISHIMA was sunk by four American aerial torpedoes on 15 November 1942.) LAFFEY was awarded the Presidential Unit Citation for her actions during the battle and three Battle Stars for her service in the Pacific. BARTON also earned four Battle Stars for her flag for Pacific actions. The other loss occurred in the Mediterranean off Cape Bungut, Algeria on 20 April 1944. LANSDALE (DD-426) was attacked by a concen-

USS BENSON (DD-421) was the lead ship in a class of 32 vessels. Their armament included a main battery of five 5-inch (127MM)/38 caliber dual-purpose guns and a pair of five-tube 21-inch (533MM) torpedo tube mounts. BENSON is camouflaged in the Graded System of Measure 22. She earned four Battle Stars for her wartime service, then was sold to Taiwan on 25 February 1954 and renamed LO YANG. This destroyer remained in Taiwanese service until 1975. (Real War Photos)

USS GLEAVES (DD-423) was one of the two 'odd sisters' fitted with round stacks, rather than the flat-sided stacks of 30 other BENSON Class ships. She was camouflaged in the Measure 22, the Graded System, in 1941. GLEAVES earned five Battle Stars for her service in the North Atlantic, Italian, Mediterranean, and French naval campaigns. (National Archives)

(Above) GLEAVES moves slowly in the ice floe while escorting a convoy to Argentia, Newfoundland on 27 February 1942. She is camouflaged in a modified Measure 12 system. Her stem must have taken quite a beating at the hands of the foot thick ice. (Real War Photos)

(Below) USS LANSDALE (DD-426) lies in Boston Harbor in 1940. She is painted in the Light Gray System of Measure 3. German Junkers Ju 88 and Heinkel He 111 bombers sank her off Algeria on 20 April 1944. LANSDALE earned four Battle Stars for her service in the Atlantic and Mediterranean. (Naval Historical Center)

trated attack of Luftwaffe Junkers Ju 88 and Heinkel He 111 bombers while escorting Convoy UGS-37. A torpedo hit LANSDALE in the forward fire room and despite efforts by the damage party the ship broke in two and sank. LANSDALE was awarded four Battle Stars for her service in the Atlantic and Mediterranean during World War Two.

Following World War Two all of the 27 surviving BENSON Class destroyers were placed in the Atlantic Reserve Fleet. All had been either scrapped or given to foreign navies by 1972, having served in and out of action for over 30 years.

Depth Charge 'K' Gun   Roller Rack

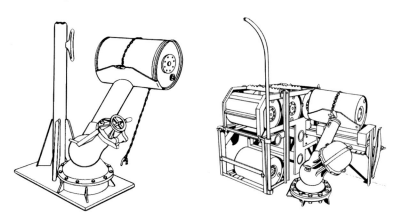

(Above) LANSDALE was camouflaged in Measure 22 on 22 October 1943. This system employed Navy Blue (5-N) just above the waterline and Haze Gray (5-H) for the remaining horizontal surfaces. Measure 22 was designed to make the ship appear farther away than it actually was. LANDSALE was painted in this measure when German aircraft sank her on 20 April 1944. Additional 20mm and 40mm anti-aircraft cannon have replaced her Number Three 5-inch gun mount and Number Two torpedo tube mount. (Floating Drydock)

(Left) USS LAFFEY (DD-459) is fitted out at the Bethlehem Shipbuilding yard in San Francisco, California on 3 January 1942. She was launched from the yard's building slip on 29 December 1941. Her 'government furnished' equipment – including the torpedo tubes, 5-inch guns, and radar and electronic equipment – were soon installed and the hull painted. A dull red anti-fouling paint was used for hull areas below the waterline. The black boot topping extended from the designer's waterline to a point six inches (15.2 cm) above the full load waterline. LAFFEY was commissioned on 31 March 1942 and immediately joined the Pacific Fleet. Japanese destroyer torpedoes and 356mm (14-inch) gunfire from the battleship HIEI sank LAFFEY in the First Battle of Guadalcanal on 12-13 November 1942. She earned a Presidential Unit Citation for gallantry in that night engagement and three Battle Stars for her wartime service. (National Archives)

USS SAMPSON (DD-394) was a SOMERS Class Destroyer Leader that was camouflaged in the Measure 16 Thayer Blue System in 1943. This scheme consisted of Thayer Blue (5-B, approximately FS35450) and White (5-U, approx. FS37855). She was armed with six 5-inch/38 dual-purpose guns and four torpedo tubes in one mount. SAMPSON was awarded one Battle Star for her service in World War Two.

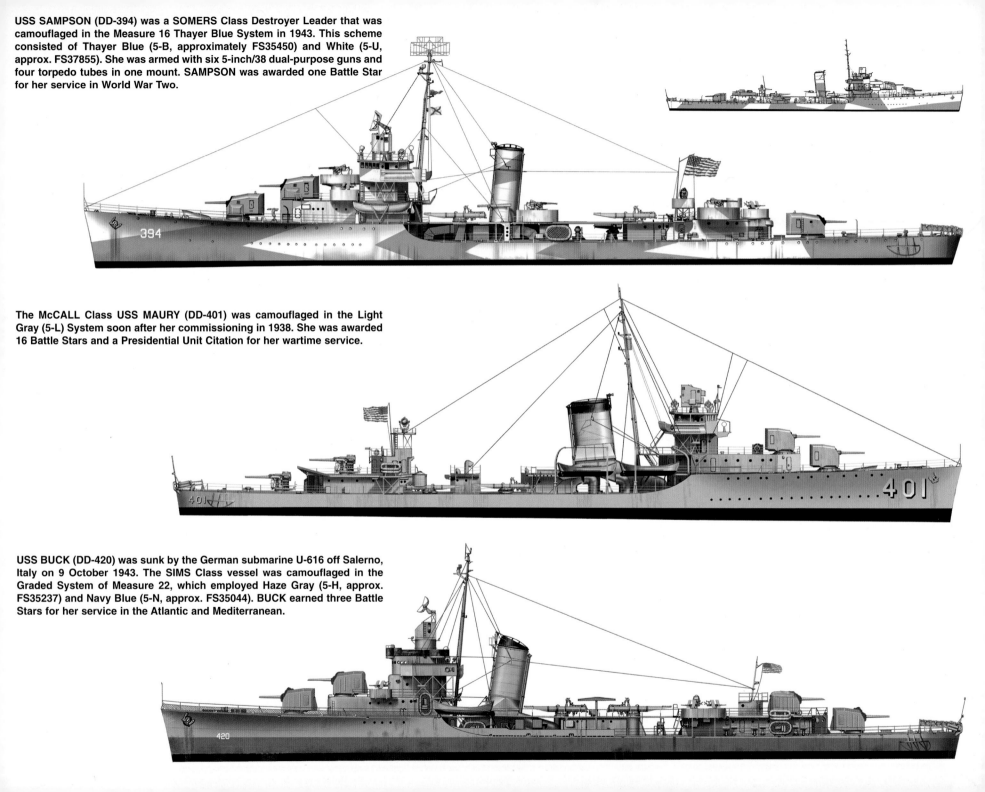

The McCALL Class USS MAURY (DD-401) was camouflaged in the Light Gray (5-L) System soon after her commissioning in 1938. She was awarded 16 Battle Stars and a Presidential Unit Citation for her wartime service.

USS BUCK (DD-420) was sunk by the German submarine U-616 off Salerno, Italy on 9 October 1943. The SIMS Class vessel was camouflaged in the Graded System of Measure 22, which employed Haze Gray (5-H, approx. FS35237) and Navy Blue (5-N, approx. FS35044). BUCK earned three Battle Stars for her service in the Atlantic and Mediterranean.

USS LAFFEY (DD-459) was sunk by the Japanese battleship HIEI off Guadalcanal on 13 November 1942. This BENSON Class Destroyer was camouflaged in the overall Navy Blue (5-N) Measure 22 System. LAFFEY earned three Battle Stars for her service in the Pacific.

The LIVERMORE Class USS BUCHANAN (DD-484) was camouflaged in a Modified Measure 12R System in 1942. This scheme used Ocean Gray (5-O, approx. FS35164), Navy Blue (5-N), White (5-U), and Haze Gray (5-H). She earned 16 Battle Stars and a Presidential Unit Citation for her service in the Pacific.

USS MACOMB (DMS-23) was the former DD-458 converted to a High Speed Minesweeper in 1944. She is camouflaged in a Tropical Green System of 31/15T. This scheme employed Ocean Green (5-OG, approx. FS34227) and Navy Green (5-NG, approx. FS34128).

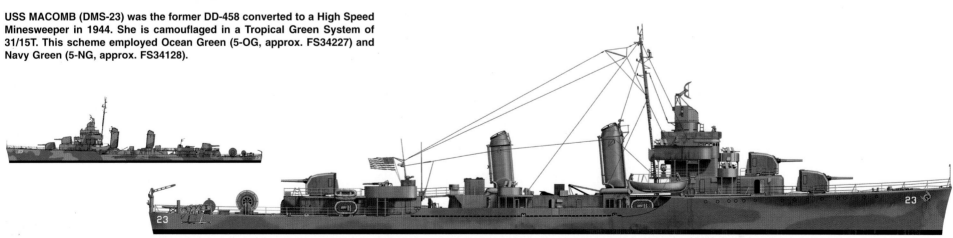

USS WOODWORTH (DD-460) is camouflaged in the Navy Blue System of Measure 21 in June of 1943. A small white hull number is painted on the bow for identification. WOODWORTH earned seven Battle Stars for her service in the Pacific. She was sold to Italy and

LAFFEY pulls alongside an unidentified heavy cruiser in the Pacific in September of 1942. She distinguished herself during the First Battle of Guadalcanal by engaging the 30,000-ton Japanese battleship HIEI in an attempt to protect the American Fleet. LAFFEY was no match for the battleship, which sank her on 13 November 1942. (National Archives)

renamed ARTIGLIERE (D553) on 15 January 1951. The Italian Navy operated this warship until discarding her in 1971. (Real War Photos)

USS FARENHOLT (DD-491) comes alongside the carrier USS WASP (CV-7) on 24 August 1942. She one of a few destroyers camouflaged in the unusual Measure 15. FAHRENHOLT was severely damaged at the Battle of Cape Esperance, near Guadalcanal, on the evening of 11-12 October 1942. She was repaired and reentered the fray in the Pacific, earning herself 11 Battle Stars. (National Archives)

USS BAILEY (DD-492) was responsible for attacking the Japanese heavy cruiser NACHI off the Aleutian Islands on 26 March 1943. Three 203mm rounds from NACHI heavily damaged the destroyer. BAILEY was repaired and rejoined the battles in the Pacific, earning nine Battle Stars by war's end. She is camouflaged in the Navy Blue System of Measure 21 in December of 1943. (Real War Photos)

USS BANCROFT (DD-598) is moored alongside an unidentified repair ship in the Pacific on 31 July 1945. An unidentified damaged destroyer escort is laid up along BANCROFT's port side. BANCROFT appears to have some damage to her deck in the forecastle area. She earned eight Battle Stars for her service in the Pacific. (Naval Historical Center)

USS BARTON (DD-599) is camouflaged in a modified Measure 12 system while underway in Boston Harbor on 29 May 1942. She soon sailed for the Pacific and arrived in October – in time to participate in the First Battle of Guadalcanal on 12-13 November 1942. Two torpedoes launched by the Japanese destroyer AMATSUKAZE sank BARTON in this engagement. BARTON earned four Battle Stars for her brief service in the Pacific. (National Archives)

USS BOYLE (DD-600) is camouflaged in the Medium Disruptive Light Pattern of 32/3D that many BENSON Class ships were finished in 1944. A High Frequency/Direction Finding (HF/DF) antenna is mounted on her pole mainmast, while SA air-search and SG surface search radar antennas are located on the foremast. BOYLE earned four Battle Stars for her service in the Atlantic and Pacific Theatres. (Floating Drydock)

(Above) USS MURPHY (DD-603), camouflaged in Measure 22, is secured by a towline from the battleship USS NEW YORK (BB-34). This was in preparation for underway refueling in the Atlantic as both ships head for the invasion of North Africa (Operation TORCH) in November of 1942. MURPHY also participated in the invasions of Sicily, Normandy, and Southern France, earning her four Battle Stars. (Thomas C. Edrington III)

(Above Right) USS CHAMPLAIN (DD-601) was camouflaged in the Graded System of Measure 22, with an unusually high painted boot topping, while undergoing sea trials in September of 1942. The black boot topping was painted just above the waterline and hid oil stains on the hull. CHAMPAIN was responsible for sinking the German submarine U-130 with depth charges on 12 March 1943. She attacked U-856 with depth charges on 7 April 1944. CHAMPLAIN rammed the U-Boat when it surfaced, which sent U-856 to the bottom of the Atlantic. CHAMPLAIN earned six Battle Stars for her service in the Atlantic and Pacific. (National Archives)

(Right) USS CALDWELL (DD-605) comes alongside the escort carrier USS MANILA BAY (CVE-61) to take on men and mail from home. She is camouflaged in Measure 21, the Navy Blue System, and has an SC-2 radar antenna atop her foremast and an SG radar antenna just below it. A Japanese *kamikaze* (suicide aircraft) hit CALDWELL's bridge area off the Philippines on 12 December 1944. She was repaired and returned to service in the fall of 1945. CALDWELL earned eight Battle Stars for her service in the Pacific. (Real War Photos)

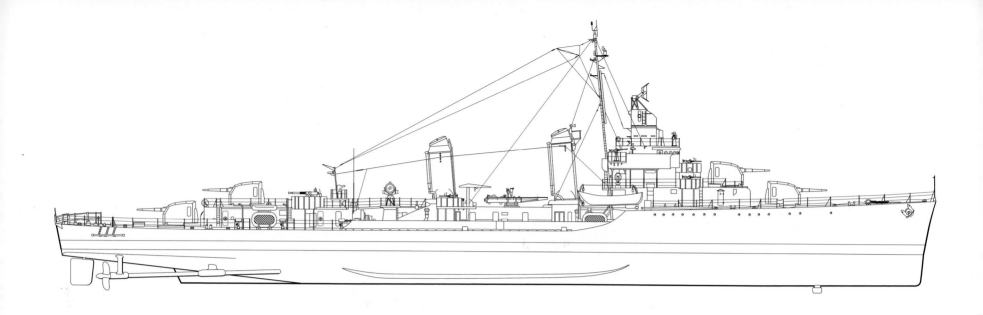

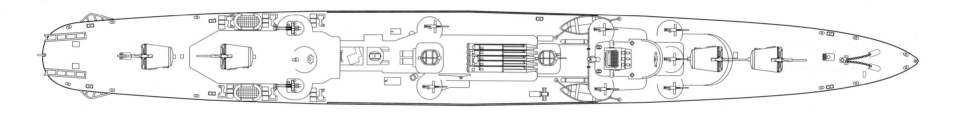

USS BENSON (DD-421) Specifications

Overall Length:................348 feet 1.81 inches (106.1 м)
Beam:................................36 feet 2.13 inches (11 м)
Draft:..............................13 feet 4.5 inches (4.1 м) at Full Load
Standard Displacement:..1840 tons (1870 мт)
Full Load Displacement:..2474 tons (2514 мт)
Machinery:........................Four Babcock & Wilcox boilers and two
Westinghouse turbines generating 50,000
sʜᴘ; two screws
Speed:..............................38 knots (43.8 ᴍᴘʜ/70.4 ᴋᴍʜ)
Range:..............................5580 nautical miles (6425 miles/10,340 ᴋᴍ) at
12 knots (13.8 ᴍᴘʜ/22.2 ᴋᴍʜ)

Compliment:......................250
Armament:........................Four (originally five) 5-inch (127ᴍᴍ)/38 caliber
guns in single mounts, four 40ᴍᴍ Bofors
cannon in twin mounts, seven 20ᴍᴍ Oerlikon
cannon in single mounts, five (originally ten)
21-inch (533ᴍᴍ) torpedo tubes, two depth
charge roller tracks on the fantail and four
roller racks along the deck edges.

(Above) USS GANSEVOORT (DD-608) is camouflaged in Measure 21, the Navy Blue System, while serving in the Pacific. She was serving in the fleet protection role when a Japanese kamikaze hit her at Mangarin Bay, Mindoro, the Philippines on 30 December 1944. This attack extensively damaged GANSEVOORT and put her out of action until the end of hostilities. She earned four Battle Stars for her service in the Pacific.

(Above Right) USS KALK (DD-611) makes a high speed run close in shore and parallel to the beach on Biak Island, Netherlands East Indies (now Indonesia) on 27 May 1944. This run was taken in order that her wash might refloat the Landing Ship Tank (LST) of the 7th Amphibious Force, which became stranded on the beach due to a falling tide. KALK is camouflaged in Measure 21. She earned eight Battle Stars for her Pacific service. (Real War Photos)

(Right) USS LAUB (DD-613) is camouflaged in the Graded System of Measure 22 in 1944. A small round life ring is mounted on the starboard bridge wing, per regulations. White depth markings painted on the bow give the number of feet above the waterline. LAUB earned four Battle Stars for her service in the Atlantic. (Naval Historical Center)

KALK prepares to stand out of Bethlehem Steel Shipbuilding, San Francisco, California on 28 October 1942 – 11 days after her commissioning ceremonies. She has an SG surface search radar antenna mounted on her foremast. Either her SA air-search radar antenna has not been fitted or the wartime censors have removed it. A Mk 4 radar antenna is placed on her Mk 37 fire control director, which is located above her bridge. The Mk 37 provided guidance for KALK's 5-inch guns. (Real War Photos)

USS ORDRONAUX (DD-617) was the last BENSON Class ship built. Launched from Bethlehem's Fore River yard in Quincy, Massachusetts on 9 November 1942, she was commissioned on 13 February 1943. ORDRONAUX is camouflaged in Measure 22, the Graded System, on 28 February 1943. She assisted USS CHAMPLAIN (DD-601) in the sinking of the German submarine U-856 south of Nova Scotia on 7 April 1944. ORDRONAUX earned three Battle Stars for her service in the Atlantic. (Real War Photos)

LIVERMORE Class of 1938-1941

The LIVERMORE Class represented the largest build of US destroyers since the massive 'flush decker' program during and following World War One. Sixty-four were constructed to plans drawn by naval architects Gibbs & Cox and constructed by shipyards on both coasts of the United States.

As first commissioned, the LIVERMORE Class was 348 feet 4 inches (106.2 M) in overall length and 341 feet (104 M) in length at the waterline and a beam of 36 feet (11 M). Draft was rated at 12 feet 4 inches (3.8 M) standard and 13 feet 2 inches (4 M) full war load. Displacement was 1640 tons (1666 MT) standard and 2060 tons (2093 MT) at full war load. When armament changes were made during the war displacement rose to 2395 tons (2433 MT) full war load. The normal wartime crew consisted of over 250 officers and men.

Four Babcock & Wilcox boilers provided high-pressure steam to the pair of Westinghouse geared turbines on the LIVERMORE Class. With over 60,000 available equivalent shaft horse-power (SHP), the class was rated at 38 knots (43.8 MPH/70.4 KMH) in light condition. Range was 6500 nautical miles (7485 miles/12,045 KM) at 15 knots (17.3 MPH/28 KMH) with available onboard fuel of 453 tons (460 MT). The LIVERMORE Class had the capability to refuel at sea, while underway, from a tanker or any other ship so equipped to dispense fuel.

When first commissioned armament consisted of five 5-inch (127MM)/38 dual-purpose naval guns in enclosed mounts and six water-cooled 0.50 caliber (12.7MM) machine guns. The Mk 37 radar controlled fire control director provided range bearings for the 5-inch guns. A pair of 21-inch (533MM) five tube torpedo mounts were fitted with one set between the stacks and one abaft set high on the centerline. For Anti-Submarine Warfare (ASW), a pair of depth charge roller tracks were fitted to the fantail. Also located on the fantail was either a single or dual smoke tank. War emergency measures necessitated the beaching of the number three 5-inch mount and replacing it with a pair of twin mount 40MM cannons in a raised bandstand. The number two torpedo tubes were also beached in favor of four additional 20MM cannons. Armament at the end of the war varied with some ships having all tubes removed and 40MM or 20MM cannons in their stead.

Twenty of the LIVERMORE Class were converted to High Speed Minesweepers (DMS) and served in the Pacific. By 1951, most were on active duty with the Atlantic and Pacific Fleet with a few in reserve and three scrapped. All of the High Speed Minesweepers reverted back to DD status by 1955.

Eleven of the LIVERMORE Class ships were lost during World War Two. The first came about due to a collision in the North Atlantic between INGRAHAM (DD-444) and the oil tanker SS CHEMUNG on 22 August 1942. The next three came in quick succession in the Pacific, when gunfire from the Japanese cruiser FURUTAKA and destroyer HATSUYUKI sank DUNCAN (DD-485) off Cape Esperance, Guadalcanal in the Solomons on 12 October 1942. Three days later, MEREDITH (DD-434) was sunk by a concerted Japanese air attack off San Cristobol Island, the Solomons. The next month, during the First Battle of Guadalcanal, the Japanese battleship HIEI sank MONSSEN (DD-436) adding to her total of American destroyers sunk during that great engagement.

Japanese aircraft attacked and sank AARON WARD (DD-483) off Guadalcanal on 7 April 1943. She was seriously damaged by HIEI at the First Battle of Guadalcanal on 13 November 1942. The next loss occurred in the Mediterranean, when MADDOX (DD-622) was sunk by a lone German Junkers Ju 87 Stuka dive-bomber off Gela, Sicily on 10 July 1943. It was back

The class leader USS LIVERMORE (DD-429) was built by the Bath Iron Works and was commissioned on 7 October 1940. She soon joined the Atlantic Fleet and served in the Neutrality Patrol prior to December of 1941. LIVERMORE served in both the Atlantic and Pacific and earned three Battle Stars for her wartime service. She was camouflaged in Measure 22 during the 1943-1944 time period. (Naval Historical Center)

USS EBERLE (DD-430) pulls alongside the carrier USS RANGER (CV-4) during Operation TORCH, the invasion of North Africa on 8 November 1942. The light cruiser USS BROOK-LYN (CL-40) passes EBERLE's stern. The destroyer is camouflaged in Measure 22. She earned three Battle Stars for her service in the Atlantic and Pacific. On 22 January 1951 EBERLE was sold to Greece and renamed NIKI (65); she was discarded in 1972. (National Archives)

USS KEARNY (DD-432) is moored alongside her sister USS MONSSEN (DD-436) after the German submarine U-568 torpedoed KEARNY south of Iceland on 17 October 1941. KEARNY was built by the Federal Shipbuilding Company in Kearny, New Jersey and commissioned on 13 September 1940. Both destroyers are camouflaged in Measure 22, the Graded System. (Naval Historical Center)

The Boston Navy Yard, Massachusetts completed USS GWIN (DD-433) and she was commissioned on 15 January 1941. She is camouflaged in the pre-war camouflage Measure 3, the Light Gray System. Her main battery consists of five 5-inch (127mm)/38 guns: three in enclosed mounts and two in open mounts. GWIN was also armed with a pair of five tube 21-inch (533mm) torpedo launchers. (National Archives)

to the Pacific War Zone for the next loss; this occurring in the Kula Gulf, when a Japanese 'long lance' torpedo hit and sank GWIN (DD-433) during the Battle of Kolombangara in the Solomons on the night of 13 July 1943. BRISTOL (DD-453) was the victim of a torpedo launched by the German U-371 while she was operating in convoy duty in the Mediterranean on the night of 13 October 1943. Less than a month later, on 6 November, BEATTY (DD-649) was also sunk in 'Hitler's lake' (an Allied nickname for the Mediterranean) when she was attacked by German torpedo bombers off Cape Bougaroun, Algeria.

The next loss was not caused by enemy action, but by an anti-submarine weapon that was fitted to TURNER (DD-648). The Mousetrap Mk 22 rocket projectile had been fitted between the number two 5-inch mount and the bridge area as a forward throwing weapon that had a range of approximately 300 feet (91 M). TURNER lay at anchor off of Ambrose Light, Sandy Hook, New Jersey on the morning of 3 January 1944. An explosion ripped through her forward section in the vicinity of the Number 2 gun magazine. Fire soon consumed the doomed ship and she sank within sight of the New Jersey coast with the loss of her Captain and 142 officers and men.

During the invasion of Normandy (Operation OVERLORD), GLENNON (DD-620) provided fire support to the landing troops until 8 June 1944, when she struck a German mine off of Quineville. The destroyer's stern settled to the bottom and efforts to free her the next few days did not come in time. German shore batteries soon found the hapless ship and on 10 June a barrage found the mark that eventually sent GLENNON to the bottom of the Bay of the Seine. This marked the last loss of a LIVERMORE Class destroyer during the long and hard-fought battles of World War Two.

GWIN (DD-433) pulls up alongside the carrier USS HORNET (CV-8) in April of 1942. HORNET's deck is covered with North American B-25B Mitchell bombers for the Doolittle Raid on Japan that month. GWIN later served at Midway before she was sunk during the Battle of Kolombangara on 13 July 1943. She earned five Battle Stars for her Pacific service. (National Archives)

(Above) USS MEREDITH (DD-434) is camouflaged in a modified Measure 12 off Suva, Fiji in June of 1942. Japanese carrier-based aircraft sank MEREDITH off San Cristobal Island, the Solomons on 15 October 1942, with the loss of 185 of her crew. MEREDITH was awarded one Battle Star for her single action in the Pacific. (National Archives)

(Above Right) USS MONSSEN (DD-436) stands off the Puget Sound Navy Yard, Bremerton, Washington on 7 May 1941. She is camouflaged in the Light Gray System of Measure 3. MONSSEN soon transited the Panama Canal to join the Atlantic Fleet on the pre-war Neutrality Patrol. Japanese naval gunfire sank her during the First Battle of Guadalcanal on 13 November 1942. MONSSEN earned four Battle Stars for her service in the Atlantic and Pacific. (National Archives)

(Right) MONSSEN passes guard mail to the aircraft carrier USS ENTERPRISE (CV-6) following the Battle of the Coral Sea in May of 1942. ENTERPRISE and her task force just missed this engagement between US and Japanese carriers. MONSSEN is camouflaged in a modified Measure 12 scheme of Sea Blue (5-S) and Ocean Gray (5-O) on the hull and Haze Gray (5-H) on the superstructure. (National Archives)

USS LUDLOW (DD-438) cruises off the Boston Navy Yard on 5 May 1942, camouflaged in Measure 12 modified. She flies her ship identification flags of (from top) N-November, E-Echo, T-Tango, R-Romeo from her foremast. LUDLOW earned six Battle Stars for her ser-

vice in the Atlantic. She was sold to Greece on 22 January 1951 and renamed DOXA (20). The Greeks operated this ship until 1972. (Floating Drydock)

USS GRAYSON (DD-435) stands off the Charleston Navy Yard on 17 April 1941. She is camouflaged in the Dark Gray System of Measure 1. GRAYSON participated in the Doolittle Raid on 18 April 1942 and served in the Pacific escorting convoys and acting as a radar picket ship guarding against Japanese *kamikazes* throughout the war. She earned 13 Battle Stars for her service. (National Archives)

Exhaust Stack Development

BENSON Class

Flat-Sided Funnels

LIVERMORE Class

Round Funnels

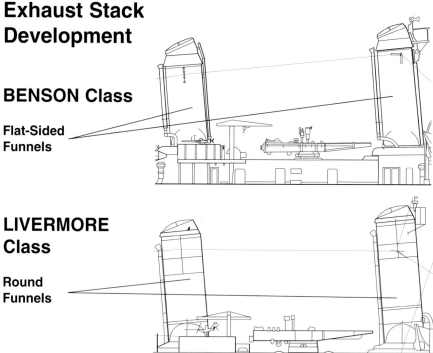

USS WOOLSEY (DD-437) steams off the Kennebec River, Maine during her builder's trials on 22 April 1941. Bath Iron Works' flag is flown from the foremast. The propeller guard protruding from the aft hull kept objects, wharfs, and piers from striking the propeller. This guard was also mounted on the port side. (US NAVY)

USS ERICSSON (DD-440) stands off Federal Shipbuilding and Drydock in Kearny, New Jersey on 11 March 1941. She is camouflaged in the pre-war Measure 3, the Light Gray System. ERICSSON, combined with the destroyer escort USS ATHERTON (DE-169) and the frigate USS MOBERY (PF-63), sank the German submarine U-853 off Block Island, New York on 5 May 1945. (Floating Drydock)

USS NICHOLSON (DD-442) was built by the Boston Navy Yard and commissioned on 3 June 1941. She stood out of New York Navy Yard to continue her service in the Atlantic on 8 January 1944. NICHOLSON is camouflaged in Measure 21, the Navy Blue System. The US sold her to Italy on 15 January 1951, when it was renamed AVIERE (D554). The Italians sank her as a target in 1975. (Floating Drydock)

WOOLSEY steams in the Atlantic in 1943. She is camouflaged in Measure 22, the Graded System. Two depth charge roller tracks are mounted on her fantail for Anti-Submarine Warfare (ASW). The charges were rolled off the stern as the ship passed over a submerged submarine. WOOLSEY aided in the sinking of the German submarine U-173 in the Mediterranean and the sinking of the U-78 and U-960 in the North Atlantic. She earned seven Battle Stars for her service in the Atlantic. (Real War Photos)

USS HAMBLETON (DD-455) sails out of Kearny, New Jersey camouflaged in Measure 11, the Sea Blue System, in 1942. Canvas tarpaulins cover her two forward 5-inch guns, which have not received their gun houses. A U-Boat torpedo hit HAMBLETON's port side off Fedala, French Morocco on 11 November 1942. She was towed to Casablanca, where she was cut in half, a 40-foot (12.2 M) section removed, and the ship welded back together and towed to Boston for repairs. HAMBLETON was responsible for sinking the German submarine U-616 in the Mediterranean on 17 May 1944. She was converted to a High Speed Minesweeper in late 1944 and redesignated DMS-20. HAMBLETON earned seven Battle Stars for her Atlantic and Pacific service.

21-Inch (533mm) Quintuple Torpedo Mount

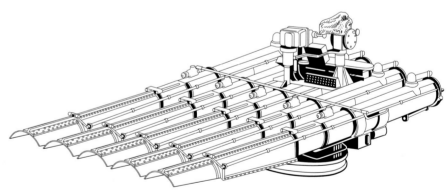

USS FORREST (DD-461) sails out of Boston Navy Yard, camouflaged in a modified Measure 12 System. She was a veteran of the invasions of North Africa, Normandy, and Southern France. FORREST was converted to a High Speed Minesweeper and redesignated DMS-24 in November of 1944. A Japanese *kamikaze* hit her off Okinawa on 27 May 1945, which put her out of the action for the remainder of the war. FORREST earned six Battle Stars for her service. (Real War Photos)

USS RODMAN (DD-456) is fitted out at Federal Shipbuilding and Drydock in Kearny, New Jersey in January of 1942. The enclosed gun houses have yet to be fitted to the 5-inch mounts and the hull is undergoing painting and rust control. Two coats of formula 84 primer were applied to the hull prior to the topcoat. Above the waterline, the second coat was formula 84D, a dark green zinc-chromate. RODMAN was converted to a High Speed Minesweeper and reclassified DMS-21 in 1944. Deployed to the Pacific, she was severely damaged by a Japanese *kamikaze* (suicide aircraft) on 1 April 1945. RODMAN was sold to Taiwan and renamed HSIEN YANG on 28 July 1955. It remained in Taiwanese service until expended as a target in 1976. (Floating Drydock)

USS EMMONS (DD-457) was commissioned at Bath Iron Works on 5 December 1941 and joined the Atlantic Fleet. She assisted in the sinking of U-616 in the Mediterranean. In November of 1944, she was converted to a High Speed Minesweeper designated DMS-22 and soon reported for duty to the Pacific. Five Japanese *kamikaze* hit and sank EMMONS off Okinawa on 6 April 1945. She was awarded the Navy Unit Commendation and four Battle Stars for her service. (Floating Drydock)

(Above Left) USS HOBSON (DD-464) steams off Charleston Navy Yard camouflaged in a modified Measure 12 in March of 1942. Wartime censors have removed her SA air-search and Mk 4 fire control radar antennas. Her search light platform was moved forward to a position immediately aft of the Number Two stack and a pair of 40MM cannon placed in its stead. (National Archives)

(Above) HOBSON was one of the few destroyers camouflaged in Measure 15 in 1943. The mottled system consisted of Navy Blue, Ocean Gray, and White in a disruptive pattern. She carries SA air search radar atop her foremast and Mk 4 fire control radar on her Mk 37 gun director. Oversize bloomers fitted to her 5-inch guns kept the weather out of her gun houses. (Real War Photos)

(Left) HOBSON's deck is covered with spent 5-inch shell casings during the bombardment of the Normandy Beachhead on 6 June 1944. The shell casings were picked up and thrown overboard as they could not be recycled. HOBSON was converted to a High Speed Mine Sweeper and redesignated DMS-26 in late 1944. She served in the Pacific for the balance of the war. (National Archives)

(Above) USS AARON WARD (DD-483) approaches the starboard side of the carrier WASP (CV-7) off the Solomon Islands on 17 August 1942. Sailors gather on her bow and along the port side to assist in the ship-to-ship operation. AARON WARD has beached her port side anchor to save weight. Japanese aircraft sank her off Guadalcanal on 7 April 1943. (National Archives)

(Above Right) USS BUCHANAN (DD-484) is secured to WASP by a towline to refuel off the Solomon Islands on 3 August 1942. She is camouflaged in a modified Measure 12R. BUCHANAN sank the Japanese submarine RO-37 west of the New Hebrides (now Vanuatu) on 22 January 1944. She had earned 16 Battle Stars and a Presidential Unit Citation when the war in the Pacific ended in 1945. This made BUCHANAN one of the US Navy's most highly decorated ships. (National Archives)

(Right) BUCHANAN was camouflaged in Measure 31/3D following a yard period at Mare Island Shipyard in 1944. She soon rejoined the Pacific Fleet for the Luzon, Formosa, and Iwo Jima campaigns and the eventual downfall of Japan. BUCHANAN was sold to Turkey and renamed GELIBOLU (D-346) on 29 April 1949; she was discarded in 1976. (National Archives)

(Above Left) USS DUNCAN (DD-485) cruises off the Federal Shipbuilding and Drydock Company on 15 April 1942. She is camouflaged in a wavy modified Measure 12 scheme. DUNCAN is equipped with the now standard main battery armament of four 5-inch/38 guns – two forward and two aft. A pair of twin 40MM Bofors cannon have replaced the Number Three 5-inch gun mount. (National Archives)

(Above) DUNCAN sails out of Kearny, New Jersey on 15 April 1942. Depth charge roller racks are fitted to her stern. After deploying to the Pacific, DUNCAN engaged the Japanese at the Battle of Cape Esperance on the evening of 11-12 October 1942. Gunfire from the Japanese cruiser FURUTAKA and destroyer HATSUYUKI hit and sank DUNCAN, with the loss of 50 of her crew. She earned one Battle Star for this single action in the Pacific. (National Archives)

(Left) USS McCALLA (DD-488) gets underway out of Kearny, New Jersey on 26 May 1942, one day before her commissioning. She is camouflaged in yet another variation of a modified Measure 12. McCALLA earned ten Battle Stars for her service in World War Two. On 27 May 1949, she was sold to Turkey and renamed GIRESUN (D-345). She remained in Turkish service until 1973.

USS LARDNER (DD-487) is camouflaged in 31/3D, the Dark Pattern System, following a refit at Puget Sound Navy Yard in 1944. She earned 10 Battle Stars for her service. LARDNER was sold to Turkey and renamed GEMLIK (D-347) on 10 June 1949. GEMLIK served with the Turkish Navy until stricken in 1981. (Floating Drydock)

Radar Antennas

SC-2

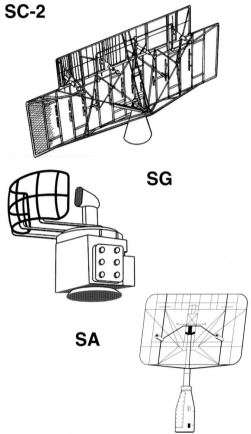

SG

SA

USS MERVINE (DD-489) undergoes a refit at the New York Navy Yard on 7 May 1943. After this refit, she sailed to the Mediterranean to participate in Operation HUSKY, the Allied invasion of Sicily. She was converted to a High Speed Minesweeper and redesignated DMS-31 in May of 1945. MERVINE earned three Battle Stars for her service. (Floating Drydock)

USS McCOOK (DD-496) cruises alongside an ESSEX Class carrier in the Pacific in 1943. This destroyer is camouflaged in Measure 22, the Graded System. McCOOK was apparently undergoing training, since no radar is installed on either the Mk 37 director or the foremast. She was converted to a High Speed Minesweeper and redesignated DMS-36 in May of 1945. (Real War Photos)

USS ENDICOTT (DD-495) is camouflaged in Measure 32/3D following a refit at Puget Sound Navy Yard in late 1944. She was a veteran of the Atlantic and Pacific Theaters of World War Two and later saw action in the Korean War. In May of 1945, ENDICOTT was converted to a High Speed Minesweeper and redesignated DMS-35. (National Archives)

USS QUICK (DD-490) stands out from the New York Navy Yard on 15 July 1942, while her officers man the weather bridge. She is camouflaged in a modified Measure 12. QUICK assisted in the sinking of the German submarine U-173 on 16 November 1942 during the Allied invasion of French North Africa (Operation TORCH). She earned four Battle Stars for her service in the Atlantic. (Floating Drydock)

USS EDWARDS (DD-619) is underway in the Caribbean during her shakedown and training cruise in 1942. She is camouflaged in Measure 22, the Graded System. Federal Shipbuilding constructed EDWARDS, which was commissioned on 18 September 1942. She earned 14 Battle Stars for her service in the Pacific. (National Archives)

Federal Shipbuilding Company delivers USS MADDOX (DD-622) to the Navy on 30 October 1942, one day before her commissioning ceremonies. This warship is camouflaged in Measure 22, the Graded System. A German Junkers Ju 87 dive-bomber sank MADDOX while on convoy duty off Gela, Sicily on 10 July 1943. She earned two Battle Stars for her Atlantic service. (Floating Drydock)

USS BALDWIN (DD-624) steams near the heavy cruiser USS QUINCY (CA-71) – carrying President Franklin D. Roosevelt – in the Suez Canal in 1945. BALDWIN is camouflaged in a Measure 32/3D scheme. She saw action in the invasions of Normandy and Southern France, earning three Battle Stars for her service. She has the flat sided bridge installed on most of the late LIVERMORE Class ships, which saved production time over the earlier rounded bridge. (Real War Photos)

Seattle-Tacoma Shipbuilding constructed USS HARDING (DD-625), which was commissioned on 5 October 1943. She is painted in camouflage Measure 22. HARDING served during the Normandy invasion of 6 June 1944. She was converted to a High Speed Minesweeper and reclassified DMS-28 in late 1944. HARDING joined the Pacific Fleet, but was severely damaged by a Japanese *kamikaze* off Okinawa on 16 April 1945. She earned three Battle Stars for her service in the Atlantic and Pacific. (Floating Drydock)

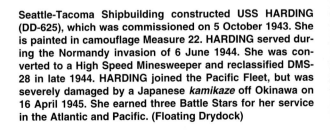

(Left) USS EARLE (DD-635, right), USS KNIGHT (DD-633), and another LIVERMORE Class destroyer undergo refit at the Boston Navy Yard in 1943. These vessels are camouflaged in Measure 22, the Graded System. Both EARLE and KNIGHT were later converted to High Speed Minesweepers and were redesignated DMS-42 and DMS-40, respectively. EARLE received two Battle Stars and KNIGHT earned four Battle Stars during the war. (Floating Drydock)

(Below) USS SHUBRICK (DD-639) cruises off the Norfolk Navy Yard on 2 March 1943. She is camouflaged in Measure 22, the Graded System. SUBRICK has been fitted with an additional 20MM Oerlikon cannon between the Number Two 5-inch mount and the bridge. She was heavily damaged off Okinawa on 29 May 1945 and stricken on 28 November 1945. SHUBRICK earned four Battle Stars for her wartime service. (Floating Drydock)

USS THORN (DD-647) stands off Federal Shipbuilding and Drydock in Kearny, New Jersey following her commissioning on 1 April 1943. She is camouflaged in a Measure 22 scheme. Wartime censors have removed her SC-2 air-search and SG surface search radar antennas for security reasons. THORN's bridge has flat sides rather than the rounded type of the earlier LIVERMORE Class destroyers. (Floating Drydock)

Mk 20 'Mousetrap' Anti-Submarine Warfare (ASW) Launcher
(Mk 22 Launcher had eight rails)

2.25-Inch (57MM) Diameter Rocket
Length: 7.2 inches (18.3 CM)
Weight of TNT warhead: 30 pounds (13.6 KG)
Average Range: Approximately 200 yards (183 M)

THORN cruises off Duncan Basin, Cape Town, South Africa during her journey home on 15 November 1945. She is camouflaged in Measure 21, the Navy Blue System. THORN served with distinction with Destroyer Squadron Nineteen (DesRon-19) in the Pacific, helping sink the Japanese destroyer ASAGUMO in the Surigao Strait, the Philippines on 26 October 1944. She earned seven Battle Stars for her Pacific service. (USS THORN Association)

47

The Class Leader USS ELLYSON (DMS-19, formerly DD-454) is camouflaged in Measure 32/22D in 1945. She was the first of 24 LIVERMORE Class destroyers converted to High Speed Minesweepers from late 1944. ELLYSON earned seven Battle Stars for her service in the Atlantic and Pacific. She was sold to Japan and renamed ASAKAZE (DD-181) in 1954. (Floating Drydock)

The Navy converted USS HAMBLETON (DD-455) into a High Speed Minesweeper (DMS-20) for service in the Pacific in November of 1944. A wire reel replaced the Number Five 5-inch gun mount and her fantail is covered with sweep gear, handling cranes, and paravanes. Her depth charge roller tracks were moved to the fantail deck edge. HAMBLETON is camouflaged in Measure 32/22D. (Floating Drydock)

Conversions to DMS

In the latter part of 1944 the US Navy began the conversion of 24 LIVERMORE Class destroyers to High Speed Minesweepers and designated them DMS-19 through 42. They were all placed in the ELLYSON (DMS-19) Class after the conversions were completed.

The conversion to DMS consisted of removing the Number Five 5-inch (127MM) gun and all torpedo tubes. The depth charge roller tracks were moved to the fantail deck edge to make room for the sweep gear. A large wire reel was placed where the 5-inch gun was normally situated. A pair of cranes used to launch and recover the paravanes were mounted on the fantail. The paravanes were used to cut the mine tethering cables; which allowed the mine to surface. Once on the surface the mine would be destroyed by surface gunfire.

The ELLYSON Class was 348 feet 4 inches (106.2 M) in length and a beam of 36 feet (11 M). Her displacement was rated at 1630 tons (1656 MT) standard and 2575 tons (2616 MT) full war load. The wartime complement was 250 officers and men. Armament was three 5-inch/38 caliber guns, a pair of the twin 40MM Bofors cannon, and seven 20MM Oerlikon cannon.

There was one loss during the Pacific War, when EMMONS (DMS-22) was sunk by a Japanese *kamikaze* ('divine wind' suicide aircraft) off Okinawa on 6 April 1945. This marked the only loss of a High Speed Minesweeper during that long conflict, although many were severely damaged by Japanese *kamikazes*. HOBSON (DMS-26) was sunk in the North Atlantic in a collision with the second carrier WASP (CV-18) in 1952.

By 1950, 20 ships remained in commission and serving with Mine Divisions in the Atlantic and Pacific Fleets. All these vessels had reverted back to destroyer (DD) status by 1955.

USS MACOMB (DMS-23, formerly DD-458) is tied up wharf side in 1946, following the end of hostilities in the Pacific. Her Jack flies at the Jack Staff, which was a common practice for US Navy ships not under power. MACOMB earned seven Battle Stars for her service in the Atlantic, Mediterranean, and Pacific. (James Diamond)

MACOMB (DMS-23) cruises in the Pacific in 1945. She is camouflaged in the Tropical Green Measure 31/15T. MACOMB was converted from a destroyer to a High Speed Minesweeper in December of 1944. Ironically, MACOMB was sold to Japan and renamed HATAKAZE (DD-182) in 1954. (Real War Photos)

USS FITCH (DMS-25) was designated DD-462 prior to her conversion into a High Speed Minesweeper in 1944. She continued to serve in that capacity during the Korean War. FITCH cruises in the Mediterranean camouflaged in Measure US-27, the former Measure 13 (Haze Gray System) in 1951. She earned five Battle Stars for her World War Two service, including invasions of Normandy and Southern France, and action in the Pacific. (W.A. Wisnowski)

The destroyer USS HARDING (DD-625) was converted to a High Speed Minesweeper (DMS-28) in late 1944. She then reported to the Pacific to aid in minesweeping around the assault beaches of Okinawa. HARDING is camouflaged in Measure 32/3D during this period. She earned three Battle Stars for her service in the Atlantic and Pacific. (Floating Drydock)

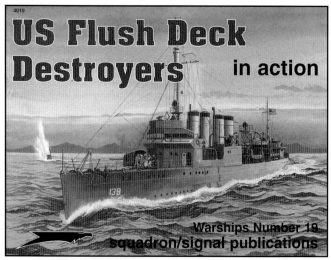